Little CHRISTMAS TREE

Barbara Anderson

Terri Einer

ISBN: 9798861411813 (Paperback)

Written by Barbara Anderson

Illustrated by Terri Einer

Book design by Misty Black Media, LLC

First edition 2023

I dedicate this book to my family,
where our Christmas memories are made.

Little Christmas Tree stood surrounded by large and beautiful evergreen trees that would be harvested soon. They would be cut and taken to be sold to homes, churches, and businesses, where they would be decorated for the holiday season. He had heard from the workers pruning the trees that they would be beautiful.

Whenever they got to Little Christmas Tree it would be time for the workers to go home, or they would take a break. Soon some of his branches were too far apart to prune nicely and his tallest peak was way too tall.

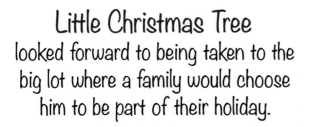

Little Christmas Tree
looked forward to being taken to the big lot where a family would choose him to be part of their holiday.

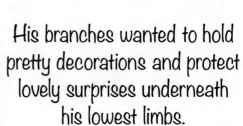

His branches wanted to hold pretty decorations and protect lovely surprises underneath his lowest limbs.

As cutting time drew near, the excitement grew, but Little Christmas Tree started to hear the other trees making fun of its uneven branches and untrimmed tall peak.

He tried not to listen.

Cutting day came with the sound of the workers cutting and loading the trees for shipping to faraway places. It was getting late, but the workers had a truck to fill. He heard them laugh as they looked at Little Christmas Tree. "Who will want this funny little tree?" they said, but they cut and threw him into the truck with the big, beautiful trees anyway.

Off they went down the highway. It was cold riding in the big truck, but he was tucked in between two large trees, so his branches were not damaged by the wind.

Soon the truck came to a stop. People came and helped the driver unload some trees, and then off they went again.

Again, the truck stopped. When only about ten trees remained, they were on the road once more. This time when they stopped, Little Christmas Tree was unloaded with the other trees.

The lot was dark. There was only a yard light and a sign, "Christmas Trees, $10.00, Leave Money Here."

The other lots they had been at were large with flashing lights and pretty signs. Those Christmas trees were very expensive. Little Christmas Tree did not want to feel unhappy, but he did feel a little sad.

Christmas Trees
$10
Leave Money Here

The next day people started coming. The sky was bright blue. Little Christmas Tree could hear voices of happy people looking for a Christmas tree. They did not stop to look at **Little Christmas Tree.**

The days passed by. Soon there were only three trees left in the dark, little lot. One couple stopped and bought two trees. They said the tall thin one would set well in their living room and the other short one would work in their recreation room. Little Christmas Tree heard this and wondered what these rooms would look like.

Christmas Trees
$10
Leave Money Here

Now **Little Christmas Tree** was alone in the parking lot. The people who owned the lot shook their heads. They told each other that no one was going to buy this funny little tree and turned off the light but left the box that said Christmas Trees, $10" outside. "We will take it down in the morning," they said.

Christmas Trees
$10
Leave Money Here

Little Christmas Tree saw the cars going by and wondered if everyone had a tree for the **holidays**.

Little Christmas Tree had begun to lose hope when a car slowed down and turned into the lot. It was Grandma and Grandpa. They had just come from visiting their grandchildren. It was two days before Christmas.

"All the Christmas trees have been sold," Grandma told Grandpa. "We have been so busy getting ready for Christmas we forgot to get our tree. I think I saw one in this parking lot when we drove by to visit our grandchildren."

When they stopped and got out of the car, they saw Little Christmas Tree. What a cute little tree!" Grandma said. "This is just the right size for our grandchildren to help decorate. I have the perfect ornaments to hang from these nicely spaced branches, and our Christmas star decoration will sit perfectly on the tall peak of the tree." Grandpa said, "It will also fit in the car". They put the money in the box. The next morning the lot people were surprised but happy to have the tree gone and $10 in the box.

Little Christmas Tree stood in the living room waiting for the grandchildren to come. The boxes of ornaments were on the floor. He heard **laughing and running.** Soon he felt warm little fingers putting family ornaments on his branches.

The little girls and boys were happy to be
helping Grandma and Grandpa.
Little Christmas Tree heard the singing
of festive Christmas carols.

A baby cried softly until his mommy rocked him to sleep. The clock ticked in the corner.

Wonderful smells of cookies baking came from the kitchen.

Little Christmas Tree was happy in the home for many days. One day Grandpa said, "We must take down the Christmas tree."

"What does that mean?" thought Little Christmas Tree.

Soon the Little Christmas Tree was outside again with the winter sun shining down on him during the day and the winter moon beaming at night. It had been a wonderful holiday season. Grandma and Grandpa hung cranberries and popcorn on Little Christmas Tree's branches. The birds perched on them and sang songs.

Little Christmas Tree was happy all winter long. When winter was over and the snow melted, Grandpa took Little Christmas Tree into the woods. He laid him down on the soft ferns and ivy.

Soon rabbits and squirrels were playing round and round under the branches that were now somewhat dry. His pine needles showered the ground around him. They would soon begin to form the soil needed to start new plants and growth.

A soft, green, moss attached to the Little Christmas Tree and grew around his decaying bark.

When spring rains and summer sun came, Little Christmas Tree relaxed. Soon his bare branches were again perches for the birds as they sang. Big, black, majestic crows would attempt to sing about memories and thoughts of the seasons of life.

Fall came, followed by winter.
Little Christmas Tree
was happy as he snuggled into the snow blanket
covering. Little mice ran under him and played.

In the spring, birds, rabbits, and squirrels would again play in the branches. For now, it was time for him to rest and dream of the children, Christmas, and new trees and plants growing in the soil.

"Merry Christmas, everyone!"
from Little Christmas Tree.

About the Author - Barb Anderson

Little Christmas Tree is author, Barb Anderson's, first children's book. Her family has many Christmas tree stories that they love to share when they gather for the holiday

About the Illustrator - Terri Einer

Illustrator Terri Einer's quirky, loose style has lent itself to several picture books. Working out of her Wisconsin studio, she loves bringing the authors words to life. You can contact the artist by visiting her website; https://www.terrieiner.com

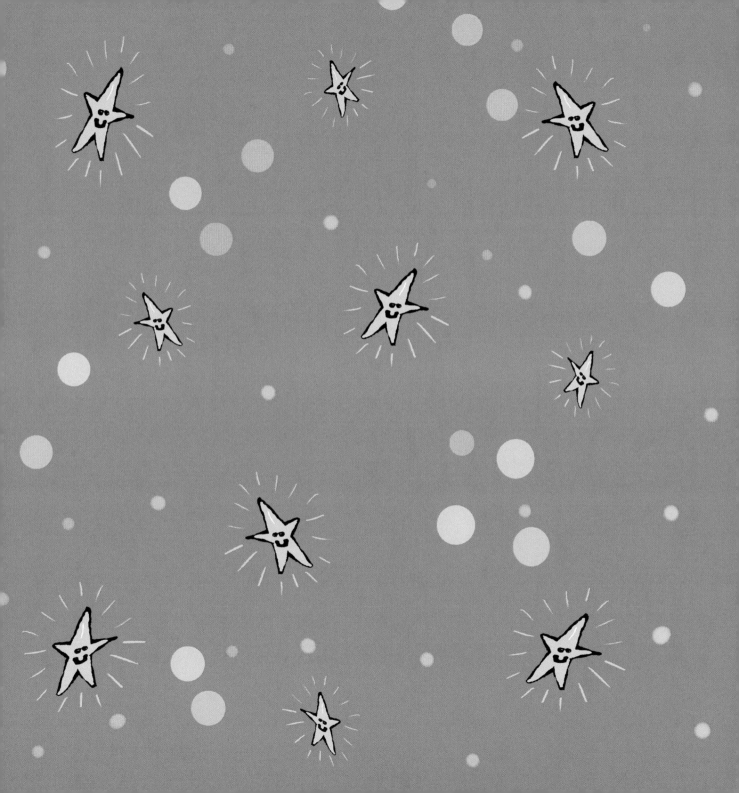

Made in the USA
Monee, IL
25 November 2023

47341740R00019